God's Health Plan

The healthy need no physician, but the sick need a doctor. Go and tell what things you have seen and heard how the blind see, the lame walk, the lepers are cleansed, the deaf hear, the dead are raised, and to the poor, the Gospel is preached.

By André Cronje

Copyright

Licensed for personal enrichment and may be used for edification and motivation. No part may be reproduced for profit or resale.

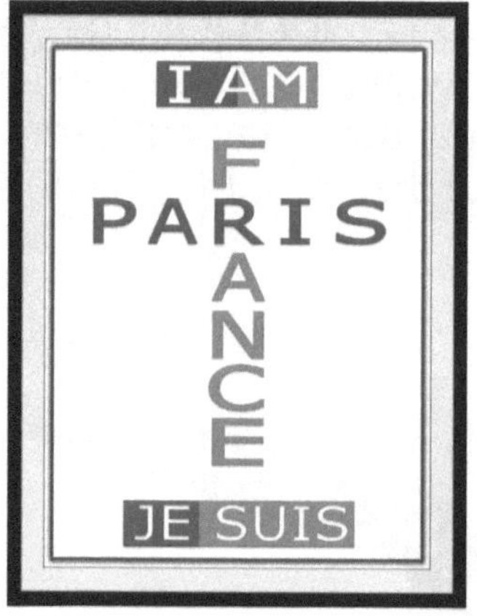

André Cronje © 2020 Copyright
Conceptual Art by André

A special honor to King James.

The Author

Andre is a South African born Huguenot descendant living in Paris, France. He is an artist, author, and owner of an online Christian clothing store. Like a potter molds his clay, so he forms and shapes his thoughts on various subjects, into conceptual art, and prophetic literature, braving social, moral, and spiritual issues with the light of Jesus Christ, who died and rose again, forgiving sins, healing the sick, and giver of eternal life, for anyone who believes and is baptized in his name.

https://andrecronje.me/

Contents

Contents   Page 5

I. Jesus Healed Them All

There was a healer in town named Jesus. Yes, he was Jewish, and a carpenter from Nazareth, but when you are sick, you don't care. Like that Roman officer from Italy, who came to Jesus and said, my servant is sick, he needs healing. God anointed Jesus with the Holy Ghost and with power, and he went to many cities doing good and healing all that were oppressed by the devil because God was with him. He healed the worst of sinners, and he healed the best of saints alike. He even raised his friend Lazarus from the dead.

He is Jehovah Rapha, the Lord who heals. Like a man who fixes his house, and a woman her home so is God at work in his creation. But God heals more than just flesh and blood. He heals nations. He heals undrinkable water, and he heals the ground that it may produce fruit. Look at what God did with the barren land of Israel. There is no such thing as incurable diseases with God. To him who believes all things are possible. Nothing is too hard for God. Jesus said, only believe and you will see the glory of God. And so he healed many because they believed.

Jesus went to many places teaching and preaching the gospel of the kingdom while healing all manner of sickness and all kinds of diseases. His fame even spread throughout Syria. And they brought to him all the sick that had various diseases and torments, and those possessed with devils, lunatics, and those that had the palsy, and he healed them all. For the healthy needs no physician, but they that are sick go to a doctor. And if the sickness gets worse, then people start looking for a specialist that would not only tell you what's wrong but also offer them a cure. But if they find no cure will they still have hope left to believe that God is able and willing to heal them?

Come to Jesus and he will heal you. God anointed him for this purpose. Sometimes he will find you lying sick in bed or sitting up in your wheelchair, or laying down drop dead in your coffin. Yip, Jesus did find them all, even a demon-possessed man who was always running naked in the hills, scaring businessmen and tourists on their way to Jerusalem. But Jesus kicked out those demons that tormented him into the local pig den and when the town council heard that the pigs committed suicide they came to Jesus begging him to leave. But the crazy man was now found clothed and in his right mind. Unfortunately, the city council was more hung over the loss of their pigs' farm, than feeling joyful over that lunatic's sweet liberty. His word is medicine to your whole body and nourishment to your bones. He renews your youth like that of an eagle. There is not one word which he has spoken that has fallen to the ground and not bearing results. Because he watches over his word, which he sends out, to do, and to fulfill it. The Lord is able and willing more than what we think.

You may say that Jesus no longer lives among us. Have you not heard, and did you not read, how after his death on the cross and his resurrection three days later, he continued to show himself alive for forty days, before he ascended to heaven in front of over 500 eyewitnesses? And at his final departure and farewell speech, he said: All power in heaven and earth was given to me to give to you that you may go to teach all nations, baptizing them in the name of the Father, the Son, and the Holy Spirit. Teaching men to observe all things whatever I have commanded you. I am with you always, to the end of the world. And these signs will follow them that believe. In my name they will cast out devils, they will speak in new tongues, they will pick up serpents, and if they drink anything deadly it will not hurt them. They will lay hands on the sick and the sick will recover. And so, after the Lord has spoken to them, he was received up into heaven and now sits on the right hand of God. And so they went forth and preached everywhere, and the Lord working with them, confirming the word with signs and wonders following.

You live in a broken world that needs constant fixing. The land in which you live and work needs healing. That's why God said: If my people who are called by my name will humble themselves and pray, I will hear and heal their land. Look at Israel, how they blossom and bloom. Once, a dessert and deserted land, now covered with fruitful trees and potential. And a booming economy means the fat of the land has returned and the sorrow of famine, war, and natural disasters have departed.

There is also healing for both mind and spirit. A broken spirit before God is precious. But an abused person is like a cracked window. But though the strong may despise the weak and wounded, God says come to me, I will be your strength. Many people are ICU cases in need of a good Samaritan to take care of their wounds and to book them into a place of care and recovery. Scars are a dim reminder of past wounds. Whether it be an injury on the playground as a child, or a battle scar defending the land. Nevertheless, some scars came by the words and deeds of loved ones or total strangers. Words that cut like a knife deeper than flesh and bones to lodge itself in the mental frame of one's soul. And when these wounds are afflicted daily, the abuse affects the person's behavior. Some are lucky to escape its effects, but others continue with the abuse mantel put on them. This will affect how you see and perceive things around you. Sexual assault can be physical or mental. It may have absolutely nothing to do with the other person, as much as their mannerism is perceived as a violation of your intimacy or domination of their private space, even though they never even touched you. Again, I hear the Lord says, bring all your cares, and burdens to him for he cares for you. Your circumstances will not have dominion over you and your past will not be your future. The balm of Gilead will bring healing, restoration, and deliverance from the effects of past and present hurts. Your famine for affection and true love ends when you enter into his presence where there is fullness of joy and healing.

There is no scientific formula for healing the sick. Thank God for your healing, because it is so easily taken for granted to credit medicine or doctors for it. God is at work and will use natural and supernatural ways to bring healing to you. Paul advised Timothy, take a little wine for your constant tummy aches. Coke helps for mine. Solomon said: Eat honey, my son, for it is good for you. The apostles also recommended that if you are sick, then go to the elders and let them anoint you with oil and pray for your healing. One time Paul prayed over handkerchiefs and when it was laid on the sick, they recovered. On another occasion, he walked by the sick, and when his shadow fell on them, they were instantly healed. Remember the Roman Officer who had great faith. He told Jesus to only speak a word, and that his servant would be healed. His servant was perhaps too sick to come to Jesus, so he approached Jesus on his behalf. He was a man under authority who also exercised authority. And when Jesus saw his faith, he marveled. Here was a gentile who was not a Jew, but he had Abraham's faith to received a miracle from God. Still, some died in hope, believing though not receiving. But God remains faithful. He is both willing and able to do what he promised. He will always be the God who heals, even if he has to raise the dead to live again. But in the new earth, the bible says, the leaves of the trees will be for the healing of the nations, where death will no longer be.

Healing may not always be felt or seen immediately. And because of that, it may be wrongly assumed that healing never took place. While skeptics look for signs, believers will receive by faith. Let him ask in prayer, believing that he received, and not doubting. Doubt will rob you of a blessing. Why do I say this? After Jesus healed ten lepers, he instructed them to go to the priest to be examined and to verify that they were clean. That was the law before a leper could come back into a community. And as they went in obedience, they were healed. But only one showed gratitude when he went back to thank Jesus for his healing. Did not all got healed, Jesus replied? Sometimes, it is in the action or going to the doctor for a second opinion that you may discover that you were healed when they prayed and laid hands on you.

You might even be lying sick in bed, like the great healing evangelist Kenneth Hagin, reading your bible, when faith suddenly enters into his heart to believe, and he got out of bed and was never sick again until his death. Sure the devil will try to come with symptoms like heart pain or short breath and tell you that you're going to die. You can believe the devil, or you can believe God's word. Faith comes by hearing and hearing by God's word. Then boldly say, devil, it is written, By his stripes, I am healed. So take your sickness and disease of me for this body is God's temple. You don't have to live sick for the rest of your life. God's word is a better life companion that will give you joy and peace. Healing comes to those who seek Christ for healing. They may have heard or read how Jesus healed someone else. Then because they believe the report they heard, they develop faith for their healing too.

II. A Suffering Healer

Believe my report. The arm of the Lord has been revealed. He grew up before you as a young plant and as a root out of the dry ground. His form of attractiveness was not beauty and desire. He was despised and rejected, a man of suffering and acquainted with illness. And with hidden faces, we despised and disregarded him. Still, it was he who has borne our illnesses and carried our suffering, yet we counted him stricken, smitten, and afflicted by God. But he was wounded for our transgressions, bruised for our iniquities, punished for our peace, and by his stripes we were healed. Like sheep, everyone went astray and turned to his own way. Thus, Jehovah laid on him the iniquity of everyone. Oppressed and afflicted he opened not his mouth. Like a lamb brought to the slaughter, and as a dumb sheep before her shearers, so he opened not his mouth. He was taken from prison and from judgment but who will declare to this generation that he was cut off out of the land of the living, and because of the transgression of the people was he stricken. His grave was with the wicked and with the rich in his death, though he did no violence, neither was any deceit in his mouth. Still, it pleased Jehovah to bruise and weaken him and to make his soul an offering for sin. He will see his seed, and he prolongs his days, and the pleasure of Jehovah will prosper in his hand. And when he sees the labor of his soul he will be satisfied. By his knowledge will my righteous servant justify many and bear their iniquities. Therefore, have I divided him a portion with the great, and he will divide the spoil of the strong. For it is he who poured out his soul unto death, and it was he who was numbered with the transgressors and bore the sin of many while making intercession for transgressors. In Exodus God revealed himself as Jehovah Rapha when He healed the entire nation all at once. There was not one feeble or sick person among them. He vowed to them to be their Physician. He gave them a free medical care and promised to heal them. God's promise was one of health and prosperity if they continued in obedience, but they often turned from him and was sorely punished. But God has send his word to heal and by his stripes you are healed.

III. Cheer Up!

And they brought to Jesus a man sick of the palsy, laying on a bed. And when Jesus saw their faith he said to the sick man, Son be of good cheer, your sins are forgiven you. But certain of the scribes said within themselves, this man is blasphemy. But Jesus discerned their thoughts and said, Why think you evil in your hearts? For what is easier? To say your sins are forgiven or to say, get up and walk? But that you may know that the Son of man has power on earth to forgive sins, (he then said to the sick of the palsy): Stand to your feet, pick up your bed and go home. And the man arose and went to his home healed, hallelujah. Jesus healed him and he still heals today. And when the multitudes saw it, they marveled and glorified God, who had given such power unto men. That is why any believer can pray and the sick will recover. Friend, if you are laying in bed sick, know this, your sins is forgiven. You can get up, make your bed, and go where ever you need to be in Jesus name. Jesus is still healing the sick and the lame, even the dead are raised.

IV. Healing In The Post

God sent his word with healing in his wings to heal. To you who fear My name will the Sun of Righteousness arise with healing in his wings. Christ was sent and anointed by God. And he sent his word and healed them and delivered them from all their destruction. A Physician empowered to heal, not by earthly powers, diplomas, or energies, but simply by the grace of God having compassion on the sick and dead men walking. Physicians and medicine do offer humanity great relief and comfort. Yet how many are wealthy enough to afford their own personal doctor? You know the battles around the world for affordable health care, especially for the poor. Some put their hopes in medicine and its rapidly increasing advances, and others put their trust in the Lord.

Have your bed of sickness crippled you and added great financial stresses to your heart and your home? With a growing list of ailments and its symptoms, some visible and others the imagination of no good physicians, the medical industry has now developed their own distribution of drugs as cures or solutions to suppress the avalanche of emotions that makes man human. The side effects have their own casualty lists. So, in a world of darkness who can see light, and who can find a cure? Your first step towards healing is to believe God is willing and able to forgive you.

Have you been sick at any time, or do you know a sick person? Then the good news is there is a cure. Thank God, he has sent his word to heal. In the gospel of John, we read how the word that was with God and was God became flesh and lived among men. The God who made you came to heal you as well. But it came with much resistance. Even though Jesus came doing good and healing sick folks, there was an establishment that was in charge of the religious ceremonies and medical certification of sick people and of sinners in desperate need for forgiveness.

The more Jesus healed the more the established religious leaders felt threatened by his gift to mankind to heal. They didn't care if people were feeling better. Nor did they care for the things of God. Fewer followers meant less power, less influence, and a smaller paycheck. But as God has sent his word so he said to his followers: Go into all the world and preach the gospel to every creature. He that believes, and is baptized will be saved, but they who believe not will be condemned. And these signs will follow them that believe. In my name will they cast out devils and speak with new tongues. They will take up serpents and if they drink any deadly thing it will not hurt them. They will lay hands upon the sick and they will recover. These were Jesus' final instructions to his disciples.

The sick, the lame, the blind, the deaf and the dumb who came to the healer, went home healed. They found hope and comfort in the teachings of Christ from Galilee and in the power of God working through him to touch the sick. His mission was clear, it was to do the will of his Father. And the will of God was to heal the sick. The power of God manifested through Jesus Christ as he cast out demons from possessed individuals, causing lame and bedridden sick to get up and walk, raising the dead, opening blind eyes and causing the ears of the deaf to hear again. This is the same Jesus who was crucified on the cross on Golgotha, the place of the skull, whom God raised from the dead. O death, where is your sting?

The first Adam was the cause of the curse, but Christ the second Adam brought a cure to the world in darkness, a light shining as he proclaimed repent for the kingdom of God is at hand Hope for healing is so much more than just a wish. It is the substance of things hoped for and the evidence of things not seen that in God, founded and carved upon the unmovable rock Jesus Christ for generations. God has sent his word who came and healed the sick. His word is medicine to all your flesh and is God's healthcare plan. However, obedience was never the requirement for healing, but to stay healthy. It is God's love and compassion to bring hope and healing to a world sick with sin and sickness. One of man's deepest desires is to have eternal youth, energy, and life. This is God's health plan for man.

V. A Woman With An Issue!

Twelve years she suffered from a condition that normally would last but only a few days. She had an issue that no man could solve. Yes, even the best doctors of her day, couldn't fix it. And like so many she kept looking until her entire fortune was spent on health care without a cure. Then she heard of Jesus of Nazareth, who went around the cities doing good and healing all that were oppressed of the devil. Many believed that God was with him because no one could do such miracles if it were otherwise. Declared unclean by the priest her movement among the clean were severely restricted and like so many people today confined to their homes, beds, and wheelchairs. But she had faith, because she said, if I could only touch the hem of his garment, I will be made whole. Her heart was alive with hope yet limited by her physical and ceremonial condition. And when Jesus came to her town she was watching him, praying for an opportunity to slip through the pressing crowd to touch him. And when the moment arrived she ready with hope and faith crawled on her knees through the crowd to reach the healer send from God. And when she got to him reached out her hand and she touched the hem of his garment as he paused for a moment. And at that very moment the healing virtue of Christ left him, and she was healed instantaneously from that spirit of infirmity.

Immediately Jesus felt the touch of faith that drained him of power. Who touched me Jesus said? What a question Jesus the disciples thought. Because the people pressed like rock fans in hope for God's touch. But when the woman realized her secret touch has drawn the public's attention, she rose from the floor and said It was me, my Lord. Jesus instantly became her high priest, as he declared to her, Woman your faith has made you whole. Her years of suffering has finally ended. She was no longer ceremonial unclean. Her healing returned to her, her freedom to socialize with friends and neighbors. This is the good news of the gospel. Not only was she healed but she was also forgiven. God wants to restore you to complete wholeness. This woman was desperate and in her search for a cure, she drained her valuable resources, like many of us today with our medical aid leaving us in debt, bankrupt, and in despair. She traveled the world, google searched and explored her options from medical research centers to alternative healing, and acupuncture. Nothing could cure her. Her issue at first seemed small but after years and heaps of medical bills, it became like Mount Everest that left many dead and scarred for life. Thus,

David said, I lift up my eyes to the hills, from where will come my help? And again, we see the response of faith as David declares with his mouth while facing his enemy. My help comes from the Lord, maker of heaven, and the earth. In another passage of scripture, David said I would have given up except that I have hope. And because of his faith, he spoke.

Doctors, healers, alternative medicines, diets, and many kinds of ritual concoctions. She tried it all saw them all, but she was one of those exceptional kinds with a rare disease variation that even send shivers down the necks of her caregivers. Some medicine seemed to have an effect, but it would not outlast her continuous flow of blood. Cures that worked for others could not set her free. The financial burden swept through her house and everyone shared the pain. Her family most concerned, yet now conditioned to her persistent condition. But she was a persistent and determined woman. If there is a God in heaven, and there is, then there must be a cure on earth. She was right, but it would come from the healer who have never performed any surgery, and who had no medical degree, nor MD, Pd, or Dr. title, before or after his name.

Whoever comes to God must believe that He is and is a rewarder of them who diligently seek him. He is the healer. Only believe and fear not. What was it that made this woman receive her healing instantly? She withdraw virtue from him like money from a cash machine, while so many others kept touching him without power flowing. Everyone was desperate to touch or to be touched by him. Did everyone who touched Jesus get healed? Everyone he touched got healed. But there were certain places where even Jesus could not perform many miracles, because of the peoples unbelief. Her touch was a touch of faith, which is the substance of the things she hoped for. She got her healing, and her health back. The substance that left Jesus' body, instantly transformed her weakened body into medical wonder. Miracles of God do not come by natural observation. Nor does God blow the trumpet on his glorious work. Jesus healed ten lepers but only one returned to thank him. Faith unseen becomes visible in our actions. Her words stand out as a proclamation of her faith. What she believed she spoke. If only I could touch the hem of his garment I will be healed. When the angel said to Mary that she was going to have a child and that he would be the Messiah, she wanted to know how it could be. And when he told her, she said: Let it be to me according to the word of the Lord. Hebrews 11 gives a list of men and women who by their faith changed the world, stopped the mouths of lions, received dead loved ones back to life, and much more amazing miracles.

Guard your heart for out of it flows the issues of life. Some issues are physical and other issues are mental , circumstantial or spiritual. Maybe you too have suffered for many years. You may have gone to many Psychiatrists, Psychologists, or Physicians, looking for health and peace of mind, but no results. You may have even spent a fortune and still haven't found good health. But if Jesus did it for this woman he can also do it for you. Jesus is alive, and the crowds are still touching and pressing him for their own healing. Press through, and touch Jesus. He has the love in him that will release the power into your situation to heal you from emotional scars, spiritual torments or physical suffering. Touch him.

VI. You're Going To Die

Besides the finest of doctors, medical staff and advances in medicine, the world still faces limitations which often results in complications or death. I am sorry to tell you, but it doesn't look good. There is nothing more we can do. You have limited time left. Get your house in order, you are going to die. The messenger of death, your beloved physician. Shock and disbelieve turn to anger. Some discover new passions, while others decide to spend their living days with pleasure.

King's crowns have enemies. Betrayal, death threats, assassin bullets, and public opinions, they all compete to clean out the office. But this message came not from the opposition or the king's physician. No, the voice that announced to the king's death was a feared man. Within a split second, the armed guard formed a shield of protection around the king. Armed and ready with swords and spears, they await the king's order. They have a license to kill on sight and to eliminate any hint of a threat against the king or crown? Still, there is a slight hesitation. For he who spoke by permission was no ordinary man. And his words are feared, and often the final clause on any matter. One can only imagine the shock and fear at the announcement: Get your house in order, you are going to die. It was a sentence of death without the possibility of healing. For when God speaks it is final, and no doctor or medicine is able to recover or heal a body whose spirit has departed. Talks of health and alternative medicine were over, and so were the king's plans after he hoped for after recovery.

A spirit of infirmity and of death took hold on the body of this king. He was about to die. It was beyond his power or the powers of medicine, doctors, and healers to keep him alive. Often people receive the same messages of despair from their beloved physicians. Sorry, there is nothing else I can do for you. Go home and say your goodbyes. Many never leave their hospital bed. Few have the misery blessing to know in advance it's the end of days for them, likewise those waiting on death row for the Day of Judgment. Each of us will react differently to the shocking news. No more years or another birthday. Go home and get your house in order or turn your face toward God and plead with him to remember you.

Hezekiah king of Judah was sick, and the prophet of God came to the king's palace to deliver a message straight from God's mouth. O king, the Lord says to you: Set your house in order, for you will die and not live. The death note was not sent by text, post, or social media. Nor was it sent by a devious person to assassin the king. No, it was handed down personally from the throne room of God to his prophet to give to the king himself. But the king's reaction was not your typical response. He did not order the execution of this holy man, nor did he faint thinking funeral preparation instead of a royal banquet. He did not seek alternative solutions or second opinions from medical experts in their field. No, he was a man who believed and feared the prophets of God even as a king. And so in the worst moment of his life, and against hope in hope believed, the king turned and facing towards the wall (of Jerusalem) he cried to God, saying, Oh Jehovah, remember me, please, how I have walked before you in truth and with a perfect heart, and have done that which was good in your sight. And he wept bitterly. And as the king's tears fell onto the marble inside his grand palace, the prophet was about to exit the king's court. At that moment God spoke again to the prophet. Go back to the king and tell him, the Lord God of David says, I have heard your prayer and I have seen your tears: See, I will add 15 more years to your days. Not only will I heal you, but I will also deliver you and this city out of the hand of the king of Assyria and defend this city. The king was no fool. For he knew God was not confused. Twice the prophet received security clearance to enter the king's presence in his private chambers, but each time he had a different message. The king didn't want to be comforted with a false prophet's blessing. So he demanded, if God truly repented of his decision, what will be the sign that I may know that I will live and defeat my enemy? Then the prophet asked him: Do you, oh king, want God to turn back the shadow of the sun, or forward it by 10 degrees? The King chose the latter and God did it according to the king's wishes. Not only did God heal the king, but he also delivered the king's people from their enemies and caused a scientific impossibility of proving that he is indeed the Highest God who lives and communicates with those who love and call upon his holy name. Wow, how awesome that God would remember kindness towards this king and the good which the king has done. With long life will I satisfy him.

Hezekiah was a good king who served God all of his days. He feared God and the man of God, the prophet who announced to him his death sentence. He didn't begged the prophet to pray for him, nor did he complained or burst out in anger toward the messenger. No! he turned to the only one who in times past saved and delivered him. Neither was his first response a helpless cry. No! with hope, he declared: God remember me, and he wept. The matter was so urgent and serious that he prayed himself for himself. When Jesus was hanging on the cross between two criminals, I heard the same words spoken by one of them. Lord, remember me when you come into your kingdom. And Jesus' immediate response was:

Today, will you be with me in paradise. Wow, wow, wow for those who believe for they will see God face to face in his glory. But woe, woe, woe unto the people who forget God and remembers him not, for there is no hope in their end. Though I go through the valley of the shadow of death, I will fear no evil.

But in a similar story, another king also laid in his bed sick. But this king ignored God and went to inquire from the best doctors he could find. Worse, he consulted from a foreign god to help him to recover from his illness. The prophet never arrived at his palace with a word from the Lord. Perhaps because God knew that this king's reaction would have resulted in the death of his beloved prophet. So God intervened, sending his prophet to meet up with the king's servants and to give them the message to convey to King Ahaziah, that his sickbed will become his deathbed never to rise again.

You will not die but live to declare the works of the Lord. Believe the prophet and you will prosper. Believe the Prophet for the word of the Lord that he speaks is life and health to all your flesh. The word of the Lord will sustain you on your bed of sickness. Death where is your sting? Where, where is your sting? Jesus said this sickness is not unto death. Then he went and raised Lazarus from the dead, Not to forget how he interrupted a funeral procession and raised a mother's child and restored a family's reunion. Death, you have no place here!

VII. Remember Me!

Three men nailed to a cross. A public spectacle for the private crimes they committed. But one was innocent, betrayed by the kiss of a friend. Only two of them would cry out to God that day. One to God in heaven, and the other, to the Lord God on the earth. The one on earth cried to the One in heaven, My God, my God, why have you forsaken me? While his fellow-sufferer next to him cried, Lord, remember me when you come into your kingdom.

One was a king despised in his land and the other a thief who got caught and brought to naught. Both needed God to save them. The one was loved by his Father in heaven, but the thief had no more credentials or credit worth of praise. But there were two thieves, one on either side of the one who was called the Christ. The one cursed himself to hell by cursing the way, the truth and the life to heaven. But his partner in crime would not have him insult an innocent man, for he saw the true identity of the one hanging next to him. We are rotten robbers to the core deserving of our pay, but he is innocent who has blessed the poor. Lord, remember me when you come into your kingdom, he whispered through his dying breath. And with an instant tweet, he got his reply: Today my friend you will be with me in Paradise.

Here this thief has confessed with his mouth that Jesus was Lord, and with his heart, he believed that Jesus was the promised King who had a kingdom, soon coming to this world. He must have heard the rumors that went around how this Jesus of Nazareth was the anointed of God, who healed the sick and preached good news to the poor. But he was too busy living up his life of crime. For money made him looked cool and for the love of money, he became a fool. Are you one of them who call on God's name in vain by living a life of crime? Or do you take God's name in vain every time you get excited about nothing? 'Omg', you may say 1000x times, yet you still don't know him who loved the world and gave his only begotten son. But death can change that in a second. For he will judge the world in righteousness and if you keep rejecting his love even on the cross when he died to take away your sin, what hope in hell do you have to get out of jail free? Hell is forever and has no fire escape. You don't want to go there.

Like the thief you too can cry to him, Lord, remember me in your kingdom. For the kingdom of God has come and will be in you. Jesus wasn't called a friend of sinners for nothing. He said whoever believes in me will never die. And even if you die, yet will you live forever. So keep praying:

Heavenly Father, hallowed be your name. Your kingdom come, and your will be done, on earth as it is in heaven. Give us our daily bread and forgive us our sins, as we forgive the sins of others. Lead us not into temptations, but deliver us from all evil. For yours are the kingdom, the glory, the power, the dominion, and the blessings forever. Amen

VIII. Demon Possessed

Jesus ignored her, and offended her, but still, she would not give up until he gave her a miracle she so desperately needed for her demon-possessed child. If you have a small coin, it has little value. But a small seed has the potential to grow into a huge tree. So, is it with faith? Little faith is needed to move big mountains, but no-faith receives nothing from God. Have you seen people possessed by devils? They do crazy things. Sometimes normal people act crazy but that's just because their emotions got the best of them. People who are demon-possessed, are often locked away from society especially when they are violent or a threat to society, but still, some roam the streets talking to the spirits that trouble them. Symptoms vary, depending on the number of devils in a person. Jesus would often cast out demons to free people from demonic oppression and possession. One such a victim was very aggressive, running naked, and scared travelers on a certain mountain path to Jerusalem. When the people bound him, he would break the chains and run away. He was totally uncontrollable. But one day Jesus came that way and delivered that man from those tormenting spirits. The results were a medical wonder. Because the man came back to his normal self, got dressed and no longer had to hide in caves away from society.

Then there was this mother whose daughter was demon-possessed. She was not going to give up fighting for her daughter's well being. She already knew that medically there was no solution. Even the advanced modern technology of this day cannot cure humans possessed by devils. Psychiatrists are powerless to offer any peace of mind to these troubled souls. Some people have found some hope in Priest performing exorcists. Because demons are subject to the name of Jesus and the power of the cross is lies in the resurrection of Christ. Her faith was stirred by what she heard, believing that Jesus could also do the same for her daughter, what he did for that man. So she searched for him and when she found him she cried: Lord have mercy on me, son of David, my daughter is harassed by a devil. But Jesus ignored her flat. But she kept begging until the disciples embarrassed asked him to send her away. You see, she was not on the priority list nor on his agenda. His father has sent him to the lost sheep of Israel and she was not Jewish. So he answered her not a word. How often have you heard people say, I prayed, and God did not answer me? And so they stop asking and walk away from God disappointed and angry. But this woman came and worshiped him and said: Lord help me. And so at this point, she could have turned back and gone home, offended, leaving bad reviews to slander his ministry. She could have lashed out and said: All men are dogs, but here she understood that dogs will not share in the riches of God's kingdom. But Lord she replied, even the dogs eat the crumbs, which fall from the master's table. And when Jesus heard her response, he exclaimed: Woman you have great faith. So be it according to your faith. And immediately her daughter was made whole that very hour.

Jesus could just speak a word, and demons would obey. This happened with a military officer whose servant was ill. As a soldier, he understood the spiritual authority and power Jesus had to command whatever he wills, and it would be done. God sent his word to heal And so the officer said to Jesus: I am not worthy that you should come all the way to my house. But just speak the word, and my servant will be healed. And when Jesus heard it, he marveled at this man's faith and said: I have not found such great faith, in all of Israel.

XIX. Healthy Foods

He rained down manna on them to eat and had given them of the corn of heaven. And men did eat angels' food. He sent them food to the full. Ps 78.24-25

Food for Champions: If you are a person who values what you are eating, then you know that certain foods have better nutrition value than regular brands. But food is not the only thing that will sustain a man in the day of sickness or adversary. If you have a strong body or mental disposition, then you may run your way back to a normal healthier lifestyle. But people need more than food to sustain them on their death beds. The word of God is food for the soul that gives life and health to both soul and body. If you want to live forever, you need to eat from the tree of life. To him that overcomes will I give to eat of the tree of life, which is in the midst of the paradise of God.

Food Approved: Eat honey, my son, for it is good for you. And this is what I do? Simple advice. No secondhand opinions or approval is necessary from the WHO, or FDA. There is a lot of advice on what and what not to eat. Friends, family members, and experts will tell you their opinions, what they have learned. But the New Testament approves all food for eating when done in faith. When you receive it with thanksgiving and prayer, he sanctifies it by his word. Peter had a vision from the Lord to eat food that was considered unclean. Jews would never eat that. It's unclean he replied. But Jesus responded: Peter, don't call unclean what I made clean, eat!

Food to Avoid: The only two food command the Jewish apostles of Jesus gave the church was: Eat not food which still has its blood in it, for life is in the blood, and eat not food offered to idols for conscience sake.

Food for Love: If what you eat is going to offend your weak faithed brother, then for love sake don't eat in front of him, what he cannot handle. Abstain for love's sake, and so fulfill God's commandment. Some are free to drink wine, while Nazarene's prefer pure juice. Paul advised Timothy to have a little wine for his constant tummy aches. You are free, but let not your freedom bring a stumbling block to your brother.

Food that Kills! Now the serpent was more subtle than any animal of the field which Jehovah God made. And he said to the woman, has God said, you will not eat of every tree of the garden? And the woman said to the serpent, We may eat of the fruit of the trees of the garden, but of the fruit of the tree which is in the midst of the garden, God has said, You will not eat of it, neither touch it, lest you die. And the serpent said to the woman, truly you will not die, die! God knows that in the day you eat of it, your eyes will be opened, and you will be as gods knowing good and evil. And when the woman saw that the tree was good for food, and that it was pleasant to the eyes, a tree to be desired to make one wise, she took of the fruit thereof and ate, and gave also to her husband with her, and he did eat. And the eyes of both were opened, and they knew that they were naked.

Food for Thought: Jesus also said that man will not live by bread alone but by every word that comes from the mouth of God. The same night in which the Lord Jesus was betrayed he took bread: And when he had given thanks, he broke it and said, Take and eat for this is my body, which is broken for you. Do this in remembrance of me. After the same manner he also took the cup, and supped, saying, this cup is the new testament in my blood. Do this as often as you drink it, in remembrance of me.

Food of Thanksgiving: Therefore, I say to you, take no thought for your life, what ye will eat, or what you will drink. Nor for your body, what you will put on. Is not life more than food, and the body than clothes? God knows you have need of these things. Serve the Lord your God, and he will bless your bread, and your water and take sickness away from you. Father, thank you that you bless my food and drink, and for taking away sickness from me, in Jesus' name, Amen. Exo 23.25

X. Live Once, Die Twice

To live once is not enough, and to die twice is too much. No one wants to die, but in Paris France, and elsewhere in the world, you can get a job, where you have no choice but to die-die, before you go home to rest. But strong men who love tough jobs, refuse to quit, and wakes up every morning, to go back to work. This die-die expression can also be found in the bible. Right at the beginning of Genesis, God said to Adam: If you eat of this tree of knowledge of good and evil, you will surely die, die. Still, Adam lived to be 930 years old, before he died. "Die" is mentioned twice here, in the Hebrew text. But translators only penned it once. For it is appointed to all men to die once, and thereafter the judgment. So, everyone dies, but not everyone dies twice.

Can man indeed die twice? The first death happens before judgment, and the second death, as a result of the judgment. Death and hell itself will be cast into the lake of fire, prepared for Satan and all his angels. But not before death has given up its dead and the sea it's dead, to appear before the White Throne Judgment Seat of Almighty God, where each man will give an account for his own works. These men both great and small, rich and poor will appear naked before their Creator and Judge without a lawyer to defend them, and without a priest to speak well on their behalf. Yes, each man will speak for himself, even the dumb, unless you have Christ as your Advocate and High Priest. And the books will be opened and whosoever name is not found written in the Lambs book of life, will be cast into the lake of fire alive, where they will burn forever, which is the second death. Thus, the second death is far worse than the first. For hell offers no fire escape and the second death is final. But whoever calls upon the name of Jesus will be saved.

A guy called Lazarus had two sisters, Martha and Mary, who believed in and loved Jesus. Then one day Lazarus became seriously ill and died. Jesus happened to be out of town, doing his Father's business. And even when he received the urgently call, he did not rush back to heal his friend and even missed the funeral. When Jesus finally returned, his friend was already dead and buried for three days. Both sisters were sadly disappointed on his return, and one of them even made a comment: Lord if you were here, my brother would not have died. True Jesus said, but he will live again. Yes, I know, at the Resurrection was her reply. But Jesus responded: I am the Resurrection and the life, whoever believes in me will never die, and even if he dies, yet will he live. So, you only live once, without God, but die twice in the end. But if you have died once with Christ, God will give you another life without end. He who believes in me will never die. Stop! Imagine this for a second. People die all the time, but Jesus said you will never die. Will, you never die, die? Wait a minute Jesus: Isn't it written that it is appointed for all men to die once? Jesus continued: Even if you should die the first death, you will live again. The second death has no power over the believer who has part of the first resurrection. Beloved, you are blessed if you hear what the Spirit of the Lord is saying to the church. Death is swallowed up in victory. The good news is, that after Jesus wept as his friend grave, he prayed to his Father in heaven. Saying, thank you, Father, that you hear me always and that this death is for your glory. So he told the people standing there with him: Roll away that gravestone. But Lord, his sisters object- ed: He is dead three days and smells like death. Yet they obeyed his instruction, for he who spoke creation into being and breathed life into Adam, became flesh stood before them, the word of God, send from heaven to earth. Lazarus, come out, Jesus shouted! Then silence. Eyes gazing at the tomb. A gasp went through the crowd as a mummy wrapped in linen came hopping out. Untie him, Jesus commanded. When Jesus raises the dead, they are still bound in their old clothes in need of a bath and a clean robe of righteousness. Proving to you that no matter how dead and bur- ied your life, dreams and hopes are, he is able.

So, when he asks you as he did to Ezekiel, can these dry bones live again? All you need to do is to believe and say Lord you know, and you will also see his glory. And when the crowd saw this, they believed in him and praised God in heaven.

I am he who was dead, Jesus said, but now I am alive. Why do you look for the living among the dead, the angels said to Mary Magdalene at the tomb of Jesus? He is not here, He has risen. And for 40 days after his resurrection, Jesus showed himself alive to his disciples and to 500 other eyewitnesses, before he ascended to heaven before their very eyes. Take comfort, he said. I will not leave you as orphans. My Comforter is with you. He will remind you of everything I said. He who died once for the sins of the world now lives forevermore and will never die again. So will you. Death has lost its sting. Christ promised the abundant life, because you believe in him, who died and rose from the dead. He is the living bread, the bread of life. Jesus is alive, and he will come again.

He was as good as dead but out of him came forth a people as many as the stars in the sky. Heb 11.20 In Ezekiel 37 God asks you a question. What will you answer him? Can this valley of dry bones live again? Lord you know. Can these dead cells in your body produce again? Lord you know. Can this bold head be covered with hair again? Lord you know. Can those missing teeth grow again?

Lord you know. Can dead rocks sing and praise God when you refuse to dance and sing when the music plays? God knows. Can limbs lost or struck dead by a stroke move again? Lord you know. Can eyes dim and blind see again? Lord you know. He was as good as dead but out of him sprang a multitude like the stars of the heavens.

Have you not heard? How a soldier killed in battle was buried into another man's grave they opened. When his body fell upon the bones in that grave, the soldier came alive and continued in war. It just happened that he was thrown into a holy grave that belonged to the prophet Elisha. You see Elisha asked for a double portion of Elijah's anointing. And when Elijah died he was short of one miracle to be double of that which Elijah did. God honored Elijah by given his faithful servant a double blessing. So is it with a lot of ministries of people who died but their works still follow them. It continues to bud and blossom just like Aaron's rod in the ark of the covenant. In the presence of God, there is only light and the light of Christ is the life of men. So, can these things be? Can a dead marriage blossom with love again? Can dead situations that are impossible with men, be possible to one who believes? Lord you know, that all things are possible to him who believes. So let it be to me.

XI. The Spiritual Body

Beauty is vain, and charm is deceitful, but a person who fears God will preserve his soul. Health charts does not prevent skinny souls. And to reduce body fats is not always the healthier solution to looking good. Remember a healthy mind and body makes a happy soul, but a spirit void of virtue is an unhealthy balance to a sound soul. If you are serious in finding a better looking you, and a healthy mindset look no more. You have found the right channel where no Botox is necessary, where you will be loved and accepted. Healing is your portion. Take it daily. In a twinkling of an eye, the corruptible will change into incorruptible, and the mortal will change into immortality. 1Cor 15.51-54

1. Your head

Blessings on your head. Prov 10.6

He anoints my head with oil. Psalms 23.5

His mischief will return upon his own head. And his violence will descend upon his own pate. Ps 7.16

But if your enemy is hungry, feed him, and if he is thirsty, give him a drink. For in so doing you will heap burning coals on his head. Rom 12.20

Indeed, the very hairs of your head are all numbered. Do not fear; you are more valuable than many sparrows. Luk 12.7

The Lord will make you the head and not the tail, and you only will be above, and you will not be underneath, if you listen to the commandments of the Lord your God, which I charge you today, to observe them carefully. Deu 28.13

You have kept me as head of the nations. 2Sam 22.44

For the husband is the head of the wife, as Christ also is the head of the church. Ep 5.23

2. Your mind

You will keep him in perfect peace, whose mind is stayed on you, because he trusts in you. Isa 26.3

He will be of quick understanding in the fear of the Jehovah. Isa 11.3

You have the mind of Christ. 1Cor 2.16

The memory of the just is blessed. Prov 10.7

My meditation of him will be sweet. Ps 104.34

He opened their minds, that they could understand the Scriptures. Luke 24:45

3. Your face

And you will lift up your face without spot, and you will be steadfast and will not fear: Job 11.15

My face is dirty with weeping, and my eyelids are like the shadow of death. Job 16.16

They look to him and were lightened, and their faces were not ashamed. Ps 34.5

And the Lord spoke face to face with Moses as a man would speak to his friend. Num 12.8

A merry heart makes a cheerful face. Prov 15.13

4. Your eyes

The eyes of the wicked will fail, and they will not escape. Job 11.20

Hear you deaf and look you blind, that you may see. Who is blind, like my servant? Or deaf as my messenger that I sent? Who is blind as he that is perfect, and blind as the Lord servant? Isa 42.18,19

The light of the eyes rejoices the heart. Prov 15.30

Moses' eyes did not dim till his death. Deu 34.7

But blessed are your eyes, for they see, and your ears, for they hear. Mat 13.6

Lord enlighten my eyes. Prov 29.13

5. Your ears

He will be of quick understanding in the fear of the Lord, and not judge after the sight of his eyes, nor reprove after the hearing of his ears. Isa 11.3

The hearing ear and the seeing eye the Lord's hands made both. Prov 20.12

He that has an ear, let him hear what the Spirit says to the churches. Rev 2.7

But they refused to hearken, and pulled away the shoulder, and stopped their ears, that they should not hear. Zech 7.11

And he began to say unto them, This day is this scripture fulfilled in your ears. Luk 4.21

He that planted the ear, will he not hear? And he who formed the eye, shall he not see? Ps 94.9

6. Your mouth

Put away from you a froward mouth and perverse lips. Pr 4.24

My mouth will show forth your righteousness and salvation. Ps 71.15

He satisfies my mouth with good things. Ps 103.5

Open your mouth and I will fill it. Ps 81.10

Fill my mouth with laughter and my lips with rejoicing. Job 8.21

The mouth of the righteous speaks wisdom, and his tongue talks of judgment. Ps 37.30

My mouth shall speak of wisdom, and the meditation of my heart shall be of understanding. Ps 49.3

The words of his mouth were smoother than butter, but war was in his heart. His words were softer than oil, yet were they drawn swords. Ps 55.21

Those things which goes out of the mouth come forth from the heart, and they defile the man. Mt 15.18

She opens her mouth with wisdom and on her tongue is the law of kindness. Prov 31.26

7. Your lips

My lips will greatly rejoice when I sing to you. _{Ps} 71.23

My lips will not speak wickedness, nor my tongue utter deceit. _{Job 27.4}

Woe is me! I am undone, because I am a man of unclean lips, and I dwell in the midst of a people of unclean lips and my eyes have seen the King, the Lord of hosts. _{Isa 6.5}

This people draws nigh unto me with their mouth, and honors me with their lips, but their heart is far from me. _{Mt 15.8}

8. Your heart

I found a man after my own heart. Acts 13.22

Keep your heart with all diligence, for out of it flow the issues of life. Prov 4.21-23

Hope deferred makes the heart sick, but when the desire comes it is a tree of life. Prov 13.12

A sound heart is the life of the flesh. Prov 14.30

Your heart will live that seeks God. Ps 69.32

God makes my heart soft. Job 23.16

Harden not your heart. Ps 95.8

Create in me a clean heart, O God; and renew a right spirit within me. Ps 51.10

9. Your spirit

God fills the weary soul and replenishes every sorrowful soul. Jer 31.25

Beauty is vain, and charm is deceitful, but a woman who fears the Lord will be praised. Prov 31.30

The spirit of man is the candle of the Lord. Prov 20.27

The same Spirit that raised Christ from the dead now lives in you. Rom 8.11

But my servant Caleb, because he had another spirit with him, and hath followed me fully, him will I bring into the land and his seed shall possess it. Num 24.14

For thou hast delivered my soul from death, mine eyes from tears, and my feet from falling. Ps 116.8

10. Your Age

Your age will be clearer than the noonday. You will shine forth like the morning. Job 11.17

You are my trust from my youth. Ps 71.5

Moses was 120 years old when he died. His eyes did not dim, nor his natural force abated. Deu 34.7

And he died in a good old age, full of days, riches, and honor. 1Chron 29:28

He renews your youth like that of an eagle. Ps 103.5

To your old age I am he, even to your grey hairs will I carry you and will deliver you. Is 46.4

You will come to your grave in a full age. Job 5:26

They shall still bring forth fruit in old age, and they will be fat and flourishing. Ps 92.14

11. Your hands

He that has clean hands will be stronger and stronger. Job 17.9

If iniquity is in your hand, put it far away, and let not wickedness dwell in your tabernacle's. Job 11.14

He will deliver the islands of the innocent, for it is delivered by the pureness of their hands. Job 22.30

Lift up your hands in the sanctuary, and bless the Lord. Ps 134.2

And let the beauty of the Lord our God be upon us. And establish the work of our hands upon us. Ps 90.17

I the Lord your God will hold your right hand, saying to you, Fear not, I will help you. Is 41.13

12. Your feet

Turn not to the right or to the left, but remove your foot from evil. Prov 4.24

Her feet go down to death and her steps take to hell. Prov 5.5

Beautiful are the feet of them who brings good news. Is 52.7

Simon Peter said to Him, Lord, then wash not only my feet, but also my hands and my head. John 13.9

How beautiful are thy feet with shoes, O prince's daughter! The joints of thy thighs are like jewels, the work of the hands of a cunning workman. Song 7.1

Her feet go down to death, her steps take hold on hell. Prov 5.5

My feet will stand in your gates, O Jerusalem. Ps 122.2

Thy word is a lamp unto my feet, and a light unto my path. Ps 119.105

13. Your bones

And he said to me, Son of man, can these bones live? And I answered: Lord God, you know. Eze 37

He will make you a new sharp threshing instrument having teeth. Isa 41.15

A sound heart is the life of the flesh, but envy rots the bones. Prov 14.30

A good report makes the bones fat. Prov 15.30

Touch his bones and flesh, and he will curse you to your face yet Job sinned not with his lips when Satan smote him with sore boils. Job 2.4-10

He will keep all your bones and not one of them will be broken. Ps 34.20

Make me to hear joy and gladness, that the bones which you have broken may rejoice. Ps 51.8

A merry heart does good like a medicine, but a broken spirit dries the bones. Prov 17.22

Let us kneel before the Lord our Maker. Ps 95.6

14. God's Body

And the magicians said to Pharaoh, this is the finger of God. Exo 8.19

With him I speak mouth to mouth, plainly and not in dark speeches. And he saw the Lord's silhouette. Num 12.8

He endured, as seeing Him who is unseen. Heb 11.27

O Lord God! I have seen the angel of the Lord, face to face. Jud 6.22

Manoah said to his wife, We will surely die, for we have seen God. Jud 13.22

Pity me for the hand of God has touched me. Job 19.21

Remove your stroke away from me. For I am consumed by the blow of your hand. Ps 39.10

The eyes of the Lord are on them that fear him. Ps 33.18,19

And the fourth person with them in the furnace is like the Son of God. Dan 3.25

He put all things in subjection under His feet, and gave Him as head over all things to the church. Ep 1.22

Christ is the head of man, and the man is the head of the woman, and God is the head of Christ. 1Cor11.3

By the word of the LORD were the heavens made, and all the host by the breath of his mouth. Ps 33.6

His head and hair are white like snow, his eyes like fire, his feet like brass as if burned in a furnace, his voice like many waters, and his countenance as the sun shining in its full strength. Rev 1.13-16

I saw also the Lord sitting upon a throne, high and lifted up, and his train filled the temple. Is 6.1

The eyes of the Lord are upon the righteous, and his ears are open to their cry. The face of the Lord is against them that do evil. Ps 34.15

15. Body Prayer

Abba Father, thank you for beautiful feet that bring the gospel of peace. Thank you for blessing my hands as I lay them on the sick to be healed. Thank you for anointing my head with fresh oil. Thank you for opening my eyes to see your glory that fills the whole earth. Thank you for ears to hear what the Spirit of the Lord is saying to the church. Thank you for filling my mouth with good things, sharpening my teeth, and beautifying my lips with kindness. Thank you for blessing my tongue to speak as the oracles of God, and not to curse what you have blessed. Thank you for a perfect heart to love and obey you, and for the mind of Christ to know your will. I praise you, Father, that I am a member of the body of Christ, and that Jesus is the head of the church. I bless you, Father, in Jesus name, amen.

XII. A Perfect Heart

I felt ill and went to see the doctor. Many tests were done to try and find the problem. But when the results came back, the doctor said to me: Your heart is perfect. Her remark stunned me. I knew her words were that from God. After God tested David's heart he concluded that this is a man after my own heart. The bible mentions others also who stood before God with a perfect heart. He searches the heart and tries the reins, to give to every man according to his ways and according to the fruit of his doings. What will your health report say after a visit to the Great Physician? In Jeremiah 17 God, deals with the heart of man. His overall conclusion is the heart of man is deceitful above all things, and desperately wicked. Who can know it? David cried to the Lord, Create in me a clean heart, and renew in me a right spirit. The wrong spirit entered ten spies that prevented Israel from possessing their promised inheritance. You may have a wrong spirit towards people and God. The arteries of your heart may be clogged with hate or unforgiveness. You may even have departed from God, and you now no longer have a passion for his presence and glory, as you use too. Life's loves and pleasures have choked your heart of divine romance and burdened you with the cares of this world. Food and things have filled the God room where the word and Spirit once dwelt richly.

Search and try our ways and turn us, Lord. In your kindness and tender mercies forgive, heal, and restore our hearts. He is a Physician and an expert on heart matters. If you have a problem you can have a heart to heart conversation with God. Let his counsel soften and purify your heart. He performed the first heart transplant when he took out the old heart of stone, and gave you a heart of flesh. It is time to draw near to God with a perfect heart, and your joy will be full. Diligently protect your heart for out of it flows the issues of life. Guard your ears and eyes from pollution. Use the sword of the Spirit to cut off those thoughts that exalt itself against the knowledge of God's word. God is love and love is the commandment that keeps a heart healthy.

XIII. Heart Problems

Circumcise your uncircumcised heart.

2. The imaginations of man's heart are evil from his youth.

3. They tempted God in their hearts.

4. Take heed, lest your heart is overcharged with surfeiting.

5. He has already committed adultery with her, in his heart, just by looking at a woman with lust.

6. A sound heart is life to the flesh but envies rotten the bones.

7. There are many devices in a man's heart, but the counsel of the Lord stands.

8. Wisdom enter into the heart of the wise.

9. Let your heart keep My commandments.

10. Write them upon the tablets of your heart.

11. Trust in the Lord with all your heart.

12. My eyes have affected my heart.

13. The meditation of my heart will be acceptable to God.

14. Perform the intents of my heart.

15. His Word in my heart is like fire.

16. The heart is awfully deceitful above all things.

17. The Lord searches the heart.

18. I will give them a heart to know Me, and they will return to Me, with all their heart.

19. I will write My law in their heart.

20. The devil steals the word out of their hearts.

21. God, make my heart soft again.

22. God knowing their hearts, purified their hearts by faith.

23. Establish your heart unblameable in holiness.

24. Blessed are the pure in heart.

25. In the uprightness of my heart, I did this.

26. Apply your heart to understanding.

27. A man's heart devises his way, but the Lord directs his steps.

28. Love one another with a pure heart.

29. Where your treasure is, there will your heart also be.

30. With perfect hearts, they willingly offered unto the Lord.

31. Keep them in the midst of your heart.

32. I have come to heal the brokenhearted.

33. My heart within me is broken.

34. A broken heart I will not despise.

35. Because of the hardness of heart God allowed Moses to issue divorce certificates.

36. My heart trembles and is moved out of its place.

XIV. How Jesus Healed

God anointed Jesus of Nazareth with the Holy Ghost and with power, and he went around doing good and healing all that were oppressed of the devil for God was with him. Acts 10.38

The same works Jesus did, you will do also. For you will receive power when the Holy Ghost comes upon you. And these signs will follow them who believe. You will lay your hands upon the sick and they shall be healed. You will speak to the dead and they will hear and obey your voice. You can do all things through Christ who strengthens you. Nothing is impossible to him who believes. It is the power of the Holy Ghost working in and through you. Some has one gift, some have another. There is no limit to the creative ways the Creator will use to perform his miracles to heal the sick. There are many ways to pray for the sick. It is not a formula by which to get perfect results every time. Even Jesus couldn't perform many miracles in his hometown because of people's unbelief, but when he went to other cities not far away many were healed and delivered.

Often Jesus would tell the people only believe. Some even cried out: Lord I believe, help me in my unbelief. Faith comes by hearing a message that addresses your need and circumstance and hearing by God's word. But when you hear a negative report from a doctor or from someone else it produces fear and hopelessness, robbing you from trusting God for a miracle. So shut your eyes and ears from those faith robbers and hold on to his promises for you. And if you believe, then you will see the glory of God.

How did Jesus heal the sick? They came to him sick and went back home healed. Their faith has made them whole. Sometimes Jesus just spoke a word without even touching that sick person. That's what happened to an Italian Officer's servant. The Officer said: Lord just speak a word and my servant will be healed. You don't need to come to my house. Besides, I not worthy to receive you. Wow Jesus marveled. Such great faith I have not seen in all of Israel. One time, Jesus spat in the dirt and took the clay to form eyes for a blind man. Did not the Lord God formed Adam from clay and breathed life into his nostrils. Sometimes he touched the sick, and other times they touched him. Jesus had compassion for the sick. Love compelled him, not money, fame, or power. No, his glory was to do the will of the Father, not his own. These signs will follow them that believe he said: In my name, you will heal the sick, cast out devil's, and even raise the dead. A few times Jesus interrupted the sorrow and pain of a funeral procession to bring back the life to the dead and joy to loved ones. It is the will of God to bring joy into your life. When Lazarus died, Jesus proved to everyone watching, that indeed he was who he said he was when he raised Lazarus to life after he was dead and buried four days. The bible is full of miracles and wonders what God has done, and what he can do again, for you if you would only believe.

Jesus was often moved with compassion and one time he even wept bitterly over the death of his friend. See how he loved him they said when they saw him weep. Oh, that God would give us such compassion and love for the sick and needy.

XV. Barren Bears

Mary was a young woman and a virgin when an angel appeared to her with the surprising news that she was going to have a baby. But how is that possible if I am still a virgin she asked? Then the angel said to her the Holy Spirit will come upon her and that she will give birth to the savior. What is impossible with man is possible with God. So Mary said let it be to me according to your words. And went to visit her relative Elizabeth who also received a miracle child because she was barren, the child in her leaped for joy when he heard the voice of Mary. Mary was about to deliver God's son and Elizabeth was about to deliver John the Baptist who would be the prophet that would pre-pare the way for Jesus' ministry. He was calling people to repentance and the sign of their obedi-ence was to be baptized. Then Jesus came and he too was baptized by John as a sign of faith. Thus, setting the example to whoever believes in him and so confess themselves to Christian should follow him in his baptism of death and be raised to life again. The four Gospels

From one super baby to another. The world's strongest man was born from the womb of a barren woman. Manoah was her husband. But an angel appeared unto her foretelling that she will have a baby blessed of God to save his people from the philistines to whom they were bound to as slaves. She is never mentioned by name and remains anonymous throughout the whole story. But she did give birth to Samson and he did judge Israel until his untimely death because of his love for Delilah.

Then there is Hannah. Her womb was shut by God. But she cried to him and made a promise that if he would bless her womb with a son, that she would offer him back to him, that he may serve God all of his life. A year later she returned to the Temple with a baby boy in her hand. And when he was 5 years old, she handed him over into the care of the priest as she has promised. And Samuel grew up in the temple and became one of the greatest and most revered prophets of God that would lead Israel for 40 years. And when Hannah gave her only begotten son back to God for his service, Eli the High Priest blessed Elkanah and his wife, and said, The Lord give you seed of this woman, for the loan which is lent to the Lord. And they went back to their home. And the Lord visited Hannah, so that she conceived, and bare three more sons and two daughters. And the child Samuel grew before the Lord.

Then there was another woman of great importance yet her name was never mentioned. She had a spirit of hospitality and when she saw a stranger passing by she invited him to stay over. Eventually, she perceived that this man was a holy man and after consulting with her husband she prepared him a room to rest there on his frequent travels. So one day the prophet Elisha wanted to repay her in kindness but she was content. His servant informed him that the woman had no child and that her husband was old. So Elisha called her and said to her she will have a baby round about the same time the following year. Shocked by what she heard, she responded, No my lord, you are a man of God, don't lie to me. And it did came to pass according to the word of the prophet that she did bear a son.

Let me share the first story from another angle. Zacharias and Elizabeth were happily married. And like most couples, they wanted to start a family. But their dreams got crushed after a medical report revealed that Elizabeth would not be able to have any children. Zacharias was a believer who petitioned God on behalf of his family, but the years went on, and they both became old. Then one day, as Zacharias was performing his temple duties as a priest, an angel appeared to him. Angels often appear to man in two forms. Disguised as a human being which the bible says, some have entertained angels unawares. Or as an angel in full glory, frightful to behold. In this case, fear not would be the proper, hello greeting. How many times have Jesus not also said that to you and me? Fear not, I have good news. Your prayer has been answered. It was the angel Gabriel, who stands in the presence of God, with a divine message. He continued to reveal the child's sex, his name, and his destiny to his father. How amazing is that? He said of Jeremiah, before I formed you in your mother's womb, I already knew you. Out of a barren womb, out of the desert came a prophet who prophesied of another, whose life and words would change the entire world.

So my friend, no matter what your age or medical report. Whose report will you believe? Let not your heart despair because of an empty womb. Hear the word of the Lord, and only believe. He opens, and he closes the wombs as in the days of old. For with God nothing shall be impossible. And as Elizabeth heard the greetings of Mary the baby in her womb leaped. And she spoke with a loud voice saying, blessed are you among women and blessed is the fruit of your womb. And blessed is she who believes, for there will be a performance of those things which were told her, from the Lord. Hallelujah, my soul magnifies the Lord. May your womb, and your home be blessed in Jesus' name. Amen.

XVI. Go And Tell

Go and tell what things you have seen and heard how the blind see, the lame walk, the lepers are cleansed, the deaf hear, the dead are raised, and to the poor, the Gospel is preached.

Since I became a Christian I saw and heard of many healing miracles. Some of those healings were unusual miracles. And I am still eager to see and hear what God is doing to this day. I used to watch videotapes of famous preachers whom God greatly used to pray for the sick. Many people were healed instantly. We now live in an age of advanced medicine, but where hope is dead miracles come alive. I can tell you from personal experiences that God is the one who does it when faith is involved. There were many times when doubt and unbelief robbed me from a sure miracle. Sin also may have been the cause of my ailments. But because of his faithfulness and mercies, I was not consumed. But sometimes I have more faith praying for myself than what I have in the faithless prayers of others. Having said this, the word does encourage us to ask the elders of the church to anoint us with oil and pray for the sick. The church must apply the power of faith and the breaker anointing of the Holy Spirit to minister healing to the sick. When miracles of healing happen it is often in such a way that one could easily doubt whether it God or not. But you live by faith. And God doesn't blow angels trumpets to announce yet another miracle. That is why it is called signs and wonders. Did he not say that you will lay your hands on the sick and they will recover. That means it could be instantaneously or in due process. I remember how someone told me of this guy in the ICU, the doctors said won't make it. After inquiry, I went to visit him and prayed. A few days later I heard that he had a recovery and was released from the hospital. On another occasion, I went with a sister from church to visit her brother in the hospital. He suddenly became ill and went into a coma. The doctors could not find what was wrong with him. I remembered we prayed together not stopped for an hour. Days later he awoke from his coma and had a full recovery.

One evening while I was sleeping, I was woken up by a loud bang outside my home. It was after midnight when I jumped out of bed and ran to see what has just happened. I arrived on an accident scene and saw what appeared to be two vehicles that have collided. One was in the middle of the road, and the second was parked in a driveway. To my horror, I discovered that it was actually one vehicle and not two. The drunk driver lost control and hit a tree at high speed, which broke the vehicle apart. I found the driver of the vehicle laying behind the front half of the vehicle in the driveway. She was laid helpless against the wall, in a half upright position, and seriously injured. I could hear her gargle for air, as blood was running down her lungs. There was no one else to help me. I knew I had to act fast. I turned her head so she could breathe more freely. Then I saw a big hole in her head where the blood was oozing out. I am no medic, but as I held her head in my hands I started to pray for her until the ambulance arrived 30 minutes later. When I prayed I said, Jesus, don't let her die. I rebuked death and declared that she will live in Jesus' name. The bible says, whatever you bind on earth will be bound in heaven, and what you loose on earth will be loosed in heaven. By faith we allow God to work in and through us. And faith pleases him. Finally, the ambulance arrived on the scene and the professionally trained personnel took care of the situation. What happened after that I didn't know until two weeks later, when someone told me that she was in a coma, at a certain hospital. I was so happy to hear that she didn't die, and decided to go and visit her. On the day that I arrived at the hospital, another miracle happened. She awoke from her coma on that very day I arrived. Praise God. It was wonderful news. I was able to talk to her and shared with her the story of what has happened. Thank God.

The most unfortunate thing that can happen to you, is that you are alone when tragedy strikes. This happened to me without warning. I was alone in an apartment when I had a stroke. I have seen many stroke survivors marred by a sudden stroke from nowhere. In an instant, one half of my body became lame. Paralyzed with fear, I remained motionless in one position. Without thinking, I started to whisper the name of Jesus, over and over again. I kept saying his name for about five to fifteen minutes until I felt life restored to my other half. Years later I would suffer a heat stroke and subsequently be hospitalized. Scans revealed scarred tissue on my brain, which alarmed the Neurosurgeon of my health condition. Doctors fervently recommend I stay on medicine for the rest of my life, to prevent another stroke. That was until I read in the bible, how God would heal me of the stroke he afflicted upon me, for my transgressions. I do believe that God can heal anyone, never to suffer another stroke or heart attack again. When you continue to walk and live in obedience to him, his health plan kicks in. When God heals you, you can throw away those labels, and medical predictions that say, you are sick for life. I prefer God's label, that says: By his stripes, I am healed. God's health plan for me is to be whole, and not to live in fear of death. I still take some painkillers for the headaches I suffer, but I no longer live in fear. Because I chose to believe God's report as my final health report.

On another occasion a mother discovered her child lying in the cot not breathing. Startled in hysteria she came running to me for help. I run to see what I could do. Instinctively I grabbed the child upside down and started to shook him, while I kept saying in the name of Jesus, over and over again. Then the boy showed signs of life, and I gave him back to his mother alive, who rushed him off to the hospital for examination. It always amazes me how miracles never seem like miracles when God does wonders. Often you hear how people died and came back to life. I also heard stories where God would wake up people to pray for a specific person. Just to find out later that in that exact time something bad had happened, but the person miraculously survived. My dad would come to me many times and say: André, I am dying. But all I knew was the name of Jesus and to pray for him. When people come to me and say, I have a pain, I don't often have the faith to pray as I want too. But in a critical situation, I sometimes just jump in and make room for Jesus to bring hope and life. I would always respond to my dad with faith by saying: Dad you not going to die. I didn't know, but God used my words to build faith and hope in him to calm his fears. It happened often, and I would always have the same reply and to pray for him. We were poor, and a visit to the doctor was not in our budget. My Dad not only also survived a stroke, but he lived an additional fifteen years in good health before he passed away. I can't thank God enough.

Did you know that Jesus healed ten lepers and only one came back to thank him? What if you prayed to God for someone you love and God heals them of cancer or some disease and you only thanked your doctor, but forgot the healer who healed. God uses any available vessel to accomplish his wonders. Sadly I have seen how some after much prayers still passed away. But the bible speaks of those who died in faith and have not obtained the promises of God. And in trying times like these, when your faith is shaken, keep trusting God. He is the great comforter and we have this hope that nothing will separate us from the love of God. Neither life nor death, riches, or poverty, or any other thing. Death has lost its sting and he who raised Lazarus from the dead lives forever. The same power that raised Christ from the dead now dwells in you. You are his workmanship created for good works. Anyone can pray for the sick in his name. Some may have the gift of unusual miracles, while others have the gift of healing. But when you are the only one around, know that God will use you to bring glory to his name. Amen.

XVII. Divine Health

Not all incurable sicknesses are fatal, or a life sentence without hope.

2. Life and death are in the power of the tongue.

3. Pleasant words bring health to the bones.

4. The spirit of a man will sustain his infirmity.

5. And the years of your life will be many.

6. The thief only comes to steal, kill, and destroy.

7. Don't wait until you can see results. Thank God today for your health and your healing.

8. I will praise Him who is the health of my countenance.

9. Man's spirit is the candle of the Lord searching the inward parts of the belly.

10. It will be health to your navel and marrow to your bones.

11. For this reason, the Son of man manifested to destroy the works of the devil.

12. God's word is life to those who find them, and health to all their flesh.

13. Elizabeth was barren. Her husband prayed, and God heard him to give them a son.

14. I will take sickness from the midst of you.

15. He sent His Word and healed them.

16. Jesus healed all sicknesses.

17. Renewing your youth like that of an eagle.

18. The curses of sickness and spells are broken in the name of Jesus. It will not trouble you anymore.

19. Leaves of the trees were for the healing of the nations.

20. When God healed the water of life flourished and there was no more death or bareness from it.

21. From the sole of their feet to the head. There is nothing sound in it. Only bruises, welts and raw wounds, not pressed out or bandaged, nor softened with oil.

22. The servant knew a man of God that could heal her master.

23. He was sick near to death, but God had mercy on him.

24. Take a present to the man of God and ask of the Lord saying, 'Will I recover of this disease?

25. If you walk in my ways, I will lengthen your days.

26. Forgiving people who have wronged you often results in your healing and peace of mind.

27. He went around doing good, not evil, healing all who were oppressed of the devil.

28. Should be converted and I heal them. Your sickness may be related to a sin or disobedience.

29. Satan smiting Job with boils. But the Lord healed him and lengthened his days in the end.

30. O spare me, that I may recover strength.

31. Be a faithful ambassador of health.

32. To you who fear My Name will the son of righteousness arise with healing in His wings.

33. Wounded for your transgression, and bruised for your sin, he was punished for your peace that by his stripes you may be healed.

34. The sick came to Jesus, and they all went home healed.

35. Love healed more people than any known cure, and hate has killed more people than any weapon.

36. Bless the Lord oh my soul and forget not all his benefits. He forgives all my sins and heals me of all my diseases.

37. Pray for the sick and believe that people will recover in Jesus name.

38. If you want to live forever, then eat from the tree of life. We die because Adam and Eve ate from the tree God said, do not eat.

39. No matter how sick a society becomes, there is always hope, healing, and God.

40. Jesus gave men the power to cast out demons and to heal all kinds of sicknesses and diseases in his name.

41. Doctors are gifts in God's health plan, as Christ is the ointment send from heaven.

42. A man's spirit sustains him in his infirmity, but a wounded spirit who can bear.

43. Before you take or give drugs to your kids for depression, ADD, or the likes, go to CCHR.org and see the human rights violations through psychiatry.

44. Ask for prayer when you are sick, for God answers the prayer of faith and will heal you.

45. All over the world people are being healed from various kinds of sickness and diseases.

46. Healing is not always instantaneous, but recovery does start with the prayer of faith and healing hands.

47. When God heals you, hold tight to your healing in faith.

48. He was wounded and bruised for our sin and peace, and so by his stripes, we were healed.

49. Pamper not your demons or chronic ailments, but shun them in Jesus name.

50. Thank God for your good health.

51. If your soul looks better than your body, you in God's hands.

52. A polluted heart causes ailments that medicine cannot cure. Many are healed as they begin to forgive.

53. Israel continues to discover incredible medical breakthroughs, the world can sing about.

54. God's word is life and medicine to all your flesh.

55. A happy face shows a merry heart, but by sorrow of the heart, the spirit is broken.

56. The light of the eyes rejoices the heart, and a good report makes the bones fat.

57. A happy heart works medicine, but a broken spirit dries the bones.

58. Cures for cancer are often ignored despite proof. But Gerson.org offers alternative non-toxic treatment for cancer and chronic diseases.

59. The hearing ear and the seeing eye are both made by the Lord's hands.

60. Man's spirit is the candle of the Lord searching the inward parts of the belly.

61. Life is in the blood. Don't eat raw meat that still has its blood in it.

62. Wisdom multiplies days and increases the years of your life.

63. Like vaccines destroy deceases, so Christ destroys sin in repented souls.

63. Words can be medicine or poison. Speak well.

64. Love mends hearts but bodies need medicine.

65. Fear of sickness acts as a magnet that affects your health in a negative way. Then faith works like a repellent allowing healing in body and mind.

66. The Bible is full of people who were cleansed from leprosy and healed from cancerous diseases.

67. For every sickness there is an antidote. In the name of Jesus be healed. By faith receive your healing.

68. The words of God are life to those that find them and medicine to all your flesh.

69. The body heals itself, but it's not the Healer.

70. Love heals the soul as medicine is for the body.

71. Keep believing God for a cure and a miracle from heaven will turn that sickness to health.

72. Anoint the sick with oil and God will heal.

73. The only sick Jesus could not heal, were those who refused to come to him for healing.

74. No matter how sick society has become, there is always hope in God's power to heal.

75. God's health plan is for those who will believe.

76. Physicians are gifts in God's Health Plan, but Christ is the ointment send from heaven.

77. One's immunity to a virus can be a medical breakthrough for someone else. Even as Christ. virgin birth made him immune to Adam's sinful nature, that became our salvation.

78. There is no medical cure for demonic ailments, but in Jesus' name, many have been delivered and healed to get back their sound mind.

79. Ask people to pray for you when you are sick, for God answers the prayer of faith, with healing.

80. All over the world people are being healed from many kinds of sicknesses and diseases. Your faith will make you whole. Only believe.

XVIII. Healing Promises

Jesus said to him, See, you have been made well, sin no more lest a worse thing come on you. John 5:14

2. Are you sick? Let the elders of the church pray for you, anointing you with oil in the name of the Lord. And the prayer of faith will save the sick, and the Lord will raise him up. And if he has committed sins, they shall be forgiven him. Confess your faults one to another, and pray one for another, that you may be healed. The effectual fervent prayer of a righteous man avails much. James 5.14-16

3. Bless the Lord, O my soul and all that is within me, bless his holy name. Bless the Lord, O my soul, and forget not all his benefits. Who forgives all my iniquities and who heals me of all my diseases. Ps 103:1

4. And the inhabitant will not say, I am sick. The people that dwell therein will be forgiven their iniquity. Is 33.24

5. I will bring health and cure, and I will cure them and will reveal to them my abundance of peace and truth. Jer 33.6

6. The Lord says: I will restore health to you, and heal you of all your wounds. Jer 30.17

7. I know the thoughts I think toward you says Jehovah, thoughts of peace, and not of evil, to give you an expected end. Jer 29.11

8. He sent his word and healed them, and delivered them from their destruction. Ps 107.20

9. Heal the sick, cleanse the lepers, raise the dead, cast out demons. Freely give, as you have received. Mat 10:8

10. I was dumb, I opened not my mouth, because you did it. Remove your stroke away from me. I am consumed by the blow of your hand. Ps 39.9,10

11. The leaves of the tree are for the healing of the nations. Rev 22.2

12. Jehovah will take away your illnesses, and put none of the evil diseases of Egypt on you. Deu 7.15

13. Jehovah will strengthen you upon your sickbed. He will make your bed in your illnesses. Ps 41.3

14. The Lord God merciful, gracious, long-suffering, and abundant in goodness and truth. Ex 34.6

15. Serve the Lord your God, and he will bless your bread, and water. He will take sickness away from the midst of you. Nothing will cast their young, or be barren in your land, and the number of your days he will fulfill. Ex 23:25-26

16. God anointed Jesus of Nazareth with the Holy Ghost and with power, who went around doing good and healing all that were oppressed of the devil. For God was with him. Acts 10.38

17. And the blood will be to you for a token on the houses where you are. And when I see the blood, I will pass over you, and the plague will not be on you to destroy you, when I smite the land of Egypt. Exo 12.13

18. Jehovah turned the captivity of Job when he prayed for his friends. Job 42:10

19. And in that day will the deaf hear the words of the book, and the eyes of the blind will see out of obscurity, and out of darkness. Is 29.18

20. The light of the moon will be as the light of the sun, and the light of the sun will be 7x times as the light of 7 days, in the day that the Lord binds up the injuries of his people and heals the stroke of their wounds. Isa 30.26

21. He gives power to the faint and to them that have no might he increases strength. Even the youths will faint and be weary, and the young men will utterly fall. But they that wait upon the Lord shall renew their strength. They will mount up with wings as eagles, they shall run and not be weary, and they shall walk, and not faint. Is 30.29-31

22. Hear you deaf and look you blind, that you may see. Is 42.18

23. Peter on this rock I will build my church, and the gates of Hades will not prevail against it. I will give you the keys of the kingdom of heaven, and whatever you bind on earth will be bound in heaven, and whatever you loose on earth will be loosed in heaven Mat 16:18-19

24. I will not die but live to declare the works of the Lord. Ps 118.17

25. We are raised up together, and made to sit together in heavenly places in Christ Jesus. Ep 2.6

26. The weapons of your warfare are not carnal, but mighty through God to pull down strong holds, and to cast down imaginations, and every high thing that exalts itself against the knowledge of God, to bring into captivity every thought to the obedience of Christ. 2Cor 10:4-5

27. Trust in the Lord with all your heart and lean not unto your own understanding. Acknowledge him in all your ways, and he will direct your path. Prov 3.5,6

28. And I sought for a man among them, that should make up the hedge, and stand in the gap before Me for the land, that I should not destroy it, but I found none. Eze 22.30

29. Are you sick? Let the elders of the church pray for you, anointing you with oil in the name of the Lord. And the prayer of faith will save the sick, and the Lord will raise him up. And if he has committed sins, they shall be forgiven him. Jam 5.14,15

30. So Abraham prayed to God. And God healed Abimelech, and his wife, and his maidservants; and they did bare children. Gen 20:17

31. If you will diligently listen to the voice of the Lord your God, and do that which is right in his sight, and give ear to his commandments, and keep all his statutes, then I will put none of these diseases upon you, which I have brought on the Egyptians. I am the Lord that heals you. Ex 15:26

32. And Moses made a serpent of brass, and placed it upon a pole. And it came to pass, that when a serpent had bitten any man, and he looked on the serpent of brass, he lived. Num 21:9

33. God is not a man, that he should lie. Neither the son of man, that he should repent. Has he said it, and will he not do it? Has he spoken, and will he not make it good? Num 23:19

34. You will walk in all the ways which the Lord your God has commanded you, that you may live, and that it may be well with you, and that you may prolong your days in the land which you will possess. Deu 5:33

35. You will be blessed above all people. There will not be male or female barren among you, or among your cattle. And the Lord will take away from you all sicknesses. And he will put none of the evil diseases of Egypt, which you know, on you, but will lay them on all them that hate you. Deu 7:14-15

36. The Lord has kept me alive, as he said, 45 years since the Lord spoke this word to Moses, while the children of Israel wandered in the wilderness. And now, I am this day 85 years old. And still I am as strong this day as I was in the day that Moses sent me. And as my strength was then, even so is my strength now for war, both to go out, and to come in. Jos 14:10-11

37. There failed nothing, of any good thing, which the Lord had spoken to the house of Israel. It all came to pass. Jos 21:45

38. And David built there an altar to the Lord, and offered burnt offerings and peace offerings. So the Lord was entreated for the land, and the plague was stayed from Israel. 1Sam 24:25

39. When heaven is shut up, and there is no rain, because they have sinned against you. If they should pray toward this place, and confess your name, and turn from their sin, when you afflicted them. Then hear in heaven, and forgive the sin of your servants, and of your people Israel. That you would teach them the good way wherein they should walk, and give rain upon the land, which you have given to your people for an inheritance. If there be in the land famine, or pestilence, blasting, mildew, locust, caterpillars, if their enemy besiege them in the land of their cities; whatever plague, whatever sickness there be. Whatever prayer and supplication is made by any man, or by all your people Israel, which you know, and every

man the plague of his own heart, and spread forth his hands toward this house. Then hear from heaven, your dwelling place, and forgive, and do, and give to every man according to his ways, whose heart you know. For you are the only One who knows the hearts of all the children of men. That they may fear you all the days that they live in the land, which you gave to our fathers. 1Kin 8:35-40

40. Blessed be the Lord, that has given rest to his people Israel, according to all that he promised. There has not failed one word of all his good promises, which he promised by the hand of Moses his servant. 1Kin 8:56

41. And Naaman the leper went down into the Jordan and dipped himself seven times according to the word of the man of God. And his skin became like that of a small child and he was clean. Then he and the people with him returned to the man of God and he said to Elijah: Now I know, that there is no God in all the earth, but in Israel. 2Kin 5. 14,15

42. Isaiah go back, and tell Hezekiah, the captain of my people, the Lord says, the God of David your father. I have heard your prayer, and I have seen your tears. I will heal you, and add 15 more years to your life. And they took a lump of figs as Isaiah said, and laid it on the boil, and he recovered. 2Kin 20:5

43. He brought them out with silver and gold, and there was not one feeble person among the tribes. Ps 105.37

44. My Lord, God of Israel, there is no God like you in the heaven, nor in the earth that keep covenant, and show mercy to your servants, that walk before you with all their hearts. 1Chron 6:14

45. Wisdom will multiply your days and the years of your life will increase. Prov 9.11

46. And the Lord listened to Hezekiah, and healed the people. 2Chron 30:20

47. Fasting God's way will cause your light to break forth as the morning, and your health spring forth quickly. Isa 58.8

48. Have mercy on me Lord, and heal me. For I am weak, and my bones are vexed even my soul Ps 6.2

49. Many are the afflictions of the righteous: but the Lord deliver him out of them all. Ps 34:19

50. The Lord will preserve you, and keep you alive. He will be blessed you on the earth. He will not deliver you to the will of your enemies. The Lord will strengthen you upon your bed of languishing. He will make your bed in sickness. Ps 41:2-3

51. Why are you cast down my soul, and why so disquieted within? I will hope in God, and praise

him, for he is the health of my countenance, and my God. Ps 42:11

52. That your way may be known on earth, your saving health among all nations. Ps 67:2

53. Lord God, I cried to you, and you have healed me. Ps 30:2

54. Because you have made the Lord your refuge, and the Most High your habitation. Therefore will no evil befall you, neither will any plague come near your dwelling. And because you have set your love on him, therefore will he deliver you and set you on high. And because you know his name, and call on him, he will answer you. He will be with you in trouble to deliver you, and honor you. With long life will he satisfy you, and show you his salvation. Ps 91

55. My child forget not my law, but let your heart keep my commandments. For length of days, and long life, and peace, will they add to you. Let not mercy and truth forsake thee, but bind them around your neck and write them on the table of your heart. So will you find favor and good understanding in the sight of God and man. Trust in the Lord with all your heart and lean not unto your own understanding. In all your ways acknowledge him, and he will direct your paths. Be not wise in your own eyes, but fear the Lord, and depart from evil. It will be health to your navel, and marrow to your bones. For she is a tree of life to them that

lay hold on her, and happy is every one that retains her Prov 3:1-8, 18

56. As a father pities his children, so the Lord pities them that fear him. Ps 103:13

57. He brought them forth also with silver and gold: and there was not one feeble person among their tribes. Ps 105:37

58. Then they cried to the Lord in their trouble, and he saved them out of their distresses. He sent his word, and healed them, and delivered them from their destruction. Oh that men would praise the Lord for his goodness, and for his wonderful works to the children of men! Ps 107:19-21

59. The Lord is gracious, and full of compassion, slow to anger, and of great mercy. The Lord is good to all and his tender mercies are over all his works. Ps 145:8-9

60. But to you that fear my name shall the Sun of righteousness arise with healing in his wings. Mal 4.2

61. My son, attend to my words. Incline your ear to my sayings. Let them not depart from your eyes, but keep them in the midst of your heart. For they are life to those that find them, and health to all their flesh. Keep your heart with all diligence for out of it are the issues of life. Prov 4:20-24

62. For by me your days will be multiplied, and the years of your life will be increased. Prov 9:11

63. You are precious in my sight and honorable and I have loved you. Therefore will I give men for you, and people for your life. Is 43.4

64. But if the Spirit of him that raised up Jesus from the dead dwell in you, he that raised up Christ from the dead shall also quicken your mortal bodies by his Spirit that dwells in you. Rom 8.11

65. In a moment, in the twinkling of an eye, at the last trump, when the trumpet will sound, the dead will be raised incorruptible, and we will be changed. 1Cor 15.52

66. And when the father of Publius, the chief man of Malta, who received Paul, and lodged him three days courteously, became sick with a fever, and of a bloody flux, Paul went to him, and prayed, and laid his hands on him, and healed him. After this, many others on the island who had diseases, came to him and were healed. Acts 28.7-9

XIX. A Blessing For You

May the Lord bless and keep you. May he cause his face to shine upon you and be gracious to you. May he lift up his countenance upon you and give you peace. May you also prosper, and be in good health, even as your soul prospers. May he bless your bread and water and heal you from every disease. May he reveal to you your inheritance you know nothing about. May your eyes see the Father's glory in everything, and may your ears hear the gentle voice of his Holy Spirit. May your name be found written in the Lamb's book of life, as you continue to love God. In Jesus name, amen.

THE END